Let Games Begin:

History of the Olympics

by Lara Bove

Editorial Offices: Glenview, Illinois • Parsippany, New Jersey • New York, New York
Sales Offices: Needham, Massachusetts • Duluth, Georgia • Glenview, Illinois
Coppell, Texas • Ontario, California • Mesa, Arizona

Every effort has been made to secure permission and provide appropriate credit for photographic material. The publisher deeply regrets any omission and pledges to correct errors called to its attention in subsequent editions.

Unless otherwise acknowledged, all photographs are the property of Scott Foresman, a division of Pearson Education.

Photo locators denoted as follows: Top (T), Center (C), Bottom (B), Left (L), Right (R), Background (Bkgd)

Cover: © Mike Blake/Reuters/Corbis; 1 © Bettmann/Corbis; 3 © Roger Wood/Corbis;4 © Jerry Lampen/Reuters/Corbis; 5 © David Gray/Reuters/Corbis; 6-7 © Bettmann/Corbis; 9 © Photo Collection Alexander Alland, Sr./Corbis; 10 © Corbis; 12 © Bettmann/Corbis; 14 © Corbis; 17 © Bettmann/Corbis; 18 © Bettmann/Corbis; 20 © Kimimasa Mayama/Reuters/Corbis; 21 © Warren Morgan/Corbis; 22 (L) © Mike Blake/Reuters/Corbis; 23 © Bettmann/Corbis.

ISBN: 0-328-13559-3

Copyright © Pearson Education, Inc.

All Rights Reserved. Printed in the United States of America. This publication is protected by Copyright, and permission should be obtained from the publisher prior to any prohibited reproduction, storage in a retrieval system, or transmission in any form by any means, electronic, mechanical, photocopying, recording, or likewise. For information regarding permission(s), write to: Permissions Department, Scott Foresman, 1900 East Lake Avenue, Glenview, Illinois 60025.

12 13 14 15 V0FL 15 14 13 12

Early Olympics

Can you imagine running a race wearing armor? That's what runners did in the first Olympic games! Early games were much different from today's games. There were chariot races and wrestling matches. There were also singing contests and soldiers who showed off their skills.

The Olympics began in Greece in 776 B.C. The events took place in Olympia. They were held every four years, like they are today. Sometimes new events were added while some were removed. The Olympic games were played for hundreds of years until they ended, for a long while, in A.D. 393.

Ancient stadium entrance, Olympia, Greece

Opening ceremony of the 2004 Olympics, Athens

A Frenchman named Pierre de Coubertin brought the Olympics back. He got other countries to take part. The modern Olympics began in 1896. The games were only held in the summer.

Today, athletes come from all over the world. The Olympics are held in a different city each time. Usually, the players cannot be paid professionals.

In the opening ceremony, the players carry a flag from their country.

The First Modern Olympics

The first modern games were held in Athens, Greece, in April 1896. It was very cold in Greece that spring, so it wasn't easy for the athletes. It even snowed during the games.

The World's Fair attracted huge crowds.

1904 Was a Year to Remember

1904 was an eventful year for the Olympics. It was the first year that the games were in America. They were held in St. Louis, Missouri. The World's Fair was also in St. Louis that year. It went from July to November. The World's Fair was a huge attraction. It was a place to see new inventions. When the Olympics became part of the World's Fair that year, St. Louis was a busy place!

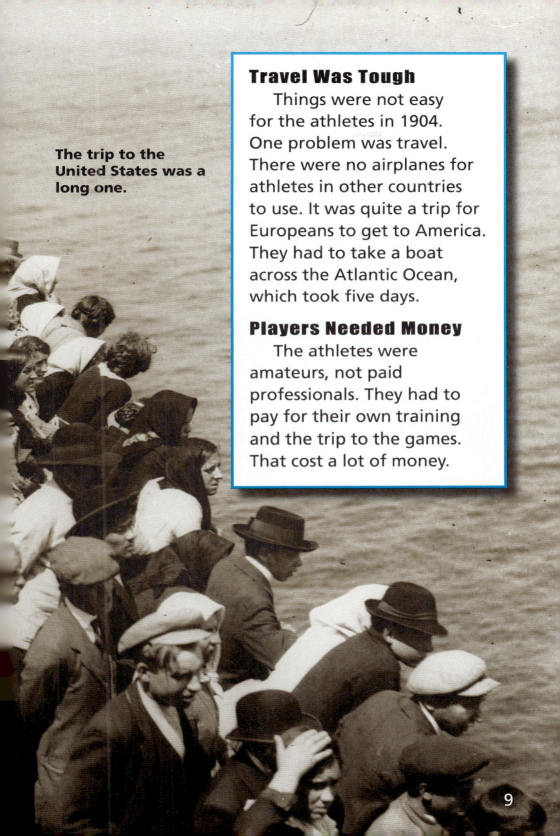

The trip to the United States was a long one.

Travel Was Tough

Things were not easy for the athletes in 1904. One problem was travel. There were no airplanes for athletes in other countries to use. It was quite a trip for Europeans to get to America. They had to take a boat across the Atlantic Ocean, which took five days.

Players Needed Money

The athletes were amateurs, not paid professionals. They had to pay for their own training and the trip to the games. That cost a lot of money.

1904: A Man with a Mission

Sometimes an athlete would raise his own money. A man from Cuba named Felix Carvajal was one such man. He was a mailman with little money. He was also a determined runner. Carvajal wanted to go to the 1904 Olympics. Without **hesitation,** he quit his job.

Now he had no job and no money. What did he do? He ran! Carvajal ran in Havana's town square, and people stopped to watch him. Having their attention, he stood on a box and told the people about his plans. He wanted to run the marathon and needed money to get to the United States. The people ended up giving him money. Felix Carvajal did this again and again until he had enough money.

Carvajal charmed people into giving him money for his trip.

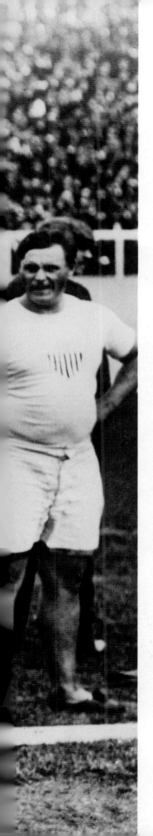

Carvajal got as far as New Orleans and ran out of money. That didn't stop him. He begged people to help him get to St. Louis. He worked to earn money and finally got to St. Louis on time.

Carvajal didn't have the right clothes for running. He only had dress shoes, long pants, and a long-sleeved shirt. Martin Sheridan was a discus thrower who helped Carvajal. He cut the sleeves off of Carvajal's shirt and made his pants into shorts.

Martin Sheridan (at left)

Poor Planning: The 1904 Marathon

The 1904 marathon was poorly planned. There was a mix of horseback riders, runners, cars, and bicycles. The horseback riders ran in front of the runners to clear the roads. The roads were not paved and horses kicked up a lot of dust. The race began

under a **bluish** sky in the early afternoon, the hottest time of day. The runners ran in the hot sun with no water and the dust had their eyes **throbbing.** Doctors rode in cars and on bicycles behind the runners and **skidded** to a halt to help those in need.

Fun Runners

Runners such as Felix Carvajal made the 1904 marathon very interesting. Felix Carvajal stopped to talk to people along the way. He spoke in Spanish and the people couldn't understand him. They liked him anyway. Everyone around him had a good time.

At one point, Carvajal stopped at an orchard to pick and eat some apples. Carvajal was **wincing** from cramps after all that food. He had to stop running and take a long break. When the cramps got better, he started running again. Somehow, he finished the race in fourth place!

The most amazing athlete of the 1904 Olympics was Ray Ewry. He was a track athlete from America. He had polio when he was a child, and the doctors said he would never walk again. The young boy wanted to make his legs stronger, so he began jumping. Ewry's legs got so strong that when he went to the 1900 Games in Paris, he won first place three times! His medals were for the standing long jump, the standing high jump, and the standing triple jump. He won gold medals in the same events in the 1904 Olympics. The crowds loved him and cheered for him. He really enjoyed being in the limelight.

Gymnastics

1904 was an amazing year for **gymnastics**. George Eyser won six medals. The amazing part was that George had a wooden leg!

| George Eyser's Medals, 1904 Olympics ||||
Event	Gold	Silver	Bronze
horizontal bar			X
parallel bars	X		
vault	X		
pommel horse		X	
rings			
rope climbing	X		
club swinging			
All-around		X	

19

Today men and women compete in gymnastics. At first only men could compete in this event. They competed using the horizontal bar, parallel bars, the vault, the pommel horse, and rings. These were all used for grace and balance. Floor exercises were added in 1932 to include **cartwheels** and the **somersault.**

Medal winners in the women's 200-meter race at the awards ceremony at the Athens 2004 Olympic Games, August 26, 2004. From left, are: Allyson Felix of the U.S., silver; Jamaica's Veronica Campbell, gold; and Bahamas' Debbie Ferguson, bronze.

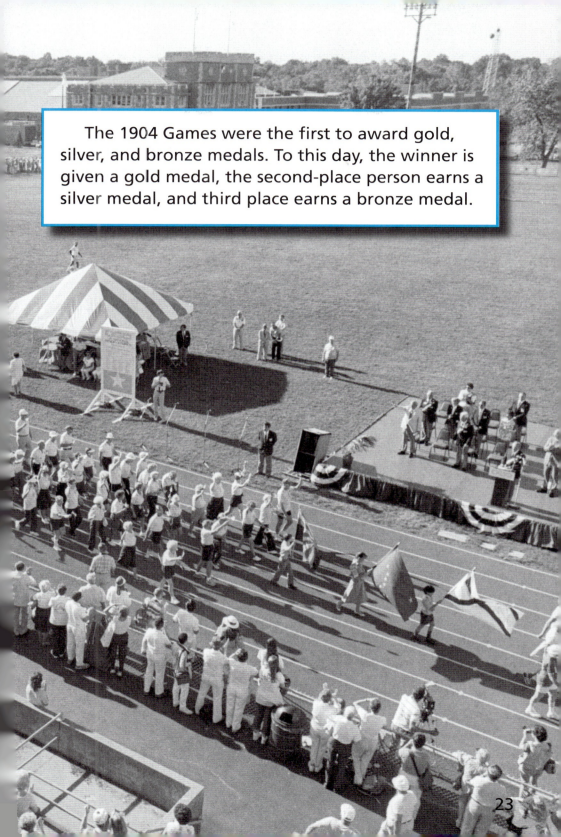

The 1904 Games were the first to award gold, silver, and bronze medals. To this day, the winner is given a gold medal, the second-place person earns a silver medal, and third place earns a bronze medal.

Glossary

bluish *adj.* having a slight or mild blue tint.

cartwheels *n.* sideways handsprings.

gymnastics *n.* exercises that use strength, agility, coordination, and balance.

hesitation *n.* a pause or doubt.

limelight *n.* the focus of attention.

skidded *v.* slid while moving.

somersault *n.* stunt performed by turning heels over head.

throbbing *v.* pulsing or aching.

wincing *v.* shrinking away; flinching slightly.

Reader Response

1. To have the "spirit of the Olympics," a competitor must have the determination to overcome obstacles. Think about Felix Carvajal's actions before and at the 1904 Olympics. How can you tell he lived up to the spirit of the Olympics? Use a graphic organizer like the one below to record your answers.

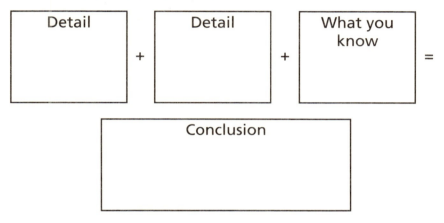

2. The runners in the 1904 marathon had to overcome many obstacles during their race. Think back to what you remember from the book and visualize these obstacles. Write down what they were.

3. Notice the word *limelight* on page 18. How does the paragraph in which it appears help suggest the word's meaning?

4. Review the chart on page 19. Why were George Eyser's accomplishments in the 1904 Olympics so extraordinary?

Suggested levels for Guided Reading, DRA™, Lexile,® and Reading Recovery™ are provided in the Pearson Scott Foresman Leveling Guide.

Social Studies

Genre	Comprehension Skills and Strategy	Text Features
Expository nonfiction	• Draw Conclusions • Graphic Sources • Visualize	• Captions • Chart • Glossary • Photos

Scott Foresman Reading Street 5.4.5

scottforesman.com

ISBN-13: 978-0-328-13559-2
ISBN-10: 0-328-13559-3